DAYS WITH DAD

A Shared Journal for Fathers and Their Children

DENNIS KNIGHT

LUCIDBOOKS

Days With Dad: A Shared Journal for Fathers and Their Children

Copyright © 2024 by Dennis Knight

Published by Lucid Books in Houston, TX
www.LucidBooks.com

ISBN: 978-1-63296-705-3
eISBN: 978-1-63296-680-3

Special Sales: Most Lucid Books titles are available in special quantity discounts. Custom imprinting or excerpting can also be done to fit special needs. Contact Lucid Books at Info@LucidBooks.com

PURPOSE

There is a two-fold purpose to creating this journal for fathers and their children. First, I know little about my dad's story. He was a great dad and very much present, but he was not intentional in sharing his story. What I know about him is primarily second-hand and from the perspective of others who could never fully know his thoughts, feelings, and dreams. If my father were still alive, he would admit that he knew very little about me, and given a second chance, he would share his story and ask more about mine.

Secondly, I am sentimental and cling to things that remind me of my father. After high school, I attempted to move halfway across the country. While he knew he had to let me go, this broke his heart. He wrote a note and left it for me to find on the kitchen table before I left. Scribbled on a half sheet of paper and with a few misspelled words, he told me he loved me and would see me soon. He even used his nickname for me, which he had used my entire life. At his death, I contemplated placing that note in his casket but rightfully decided to keep it. That note is 30 years old, and I treasure it. To this day it is the one thing of my dad's that I adore. A simple little note written in his handwriting. You can find that note in my Bible, where I will keep it for as long as I live.

Imagine possessing a collection of notes, letters, and written conversations from your dad. Notes written by him in his handwriting. Memories of moments shared. Quotes given from him that inspired you and helped navigate specific situations you grew through. Entries filled with his stories would paint a vivid picture of who he was. These notes would be treasures indeed.

This is more than just an idea for me. I have and continue to use these journals with my own children. I gifted them a blank journal with an entry from me. They were encouraged to read what I wrote and then write back to me. When they finish, they place the journal on my nightstand. They were told that there were no rules to the journal entries. They were permitted to ask or share anything that came to their mind. They were encouraged to ask any question of me and even challenge me in situations we found ourselves in. They were never pressured to write, but I would sometimes prompt them. I promised them that I would write back to them within 24 hours each time they gave the journal back to me.

This journal experience is your gift to your child. They will not only benefit in real-time as you share together on this journey but will hold onto what you both shared for years to come. It will be impossible for you not to be blessed by the entries and deepening of your relationship.

INTRODUCTION

Let me ask you a question, Dad: What are you hoping to leave your child when you leave this earth? Will you leave them money? Will you hand down a home or vacation property? Will it be memories of vacations and times you played outside with them?

As you start and commit to this journal experience, I challenge you to consider the treasure you will leave them. The end game is gifting your child a collection of stories, memories, and conversations penned in your handwriting for them to treasure long after they have grown, and you are gone.

Your child will treasure this journal more than anything else you could give them. That is a bold statement, but I believe it wholeheartedly. This gift gives them a window into your story, heart, and the journey you will lead them through from infancy to adulthood.

Dads, be creative and let this journal be anything you want but be intentional. If your child is too young to write back, then jot down memories of their early development. They will love to hear the first funny thing they said that cracked you up. Reading stories of monster blowouts and first-time tantrums thrown will show them how much you loved them long before they could even understand those words.

If your child is older, use the provided quotes/prompts and ask them what they think they mean and then follow up on those teaching moments to shape their character. They will revisit these conversations and may even smile at how their understanding has evolved over the years. They won't forget the lessons.

No matter how you decide to use this journal, remember that

long after you are gone, your child will treasure what the two of you have shared. Your impact will forever be cemented in their minds and hearts. It will be revisited more times than you can anticipate.

You already know this, Dad: they are worth it. You are their hero, so let's get it on paper and gift them this lifelong treasure.

INTRODUCE
EACH OTHER
TO THIS JOURNAL

Imagine that it is your job to introduce your dad or child
to a group of people they have never met.
Tell the group who they are through your eyes.
Be as descriptive as possible.
Use your first entry to let the world know
who your child/dad is.
Share what makes you laugh and
what you love about them.

Date: _____

"Hold yourself responsible for a higher standard than anyone else expects of you. Never excuse yourself."

—H. W. Beecher

Don't wait for people to have high expectations of you. Some people will place high expectations on you, and other's expectations will be too low. Hold yourself to the highest standards in every aspect of your life.

Go first! Expect more from yourself than anyone else ever can. It's up to you to decide what you will accept from yourself. Aim high!

"Simply wanting something is no great accomplishment."

Everyone wants to be a winner, drive the coolest car, be physically fit, become a top-level athlete, earn lots of money, and an endless list of other accomplishments. Simply wanting those things accomplishes nothing! Nothing is accomplished by wishing.

Write out all your dreams. Include all the things you want to accomplish and wish to acquire. Do you dream of going to college? Will you own your own business? Will you have a family? Will you travel and see the world? List all the places you dream of going, and then work out your plans to make them a reality.

Remember this: Most people die with a list of wishes longer than their list of memories. Don't just wish for things; go after those dreams.

Date: _____

"A man of integrity walks securely, but he who takes crooked paths will be found out."
—Proverbs 10:19 (NIV)

Integrity is like having a compass and knowing how to use it. A compass is the most accurate way to get from one place to another. It gives a person direction and tells him which way to walk. Integrity is knowing what is right and having the courage to do that right thing even when it's difficult. What are some of the areas in life where integrity is necessary?

"The Wright Brothers didn't wait until they had a pilot's license."

The Wright brothers created the first airplane. They did this before they had a pilot's license. They didn't wait for something to be created; they had a dream and made it a reality.

Your dreams are real, and they are meant to change the world. Don't wait for permission to make those dreams a reality. Henry Ford, the inventor of the first automobile, once said that if he had asked people what they wanted, they would have said they wanted a faster horse. Instead, he made his dream come true and created something the world had never seen before. He created the automobile. If you have a vision, don't wait for permission. Make your vision a reality even if everyone else can't see or understand what you are giving this world. How do you dream of changing the world?

"Kindness is loaning someone your strength instead of reminding them of their weakness."

There is a story of a stunt pilot who trusted a young mechanic to fuel his plane before an event. The young man carelessly put the wrong fuel in the aircraft. This caused the plane to shut down mid-performance, placing the pilot in danger of crashing his airplane.

The pilot was rightfully shaken and upset. He could have lost his temper with the young mechanic, but when he witnessed the remorse and fear in the young man's eyes, the pilot asked him, "Do you think you will ever make that mistake again?" The young man promised to never make that mistake again. The pilot went out of his way to make sure that the same young mechanic was responsible for fueling his plane before the next event.

That is loaning someone your kindness when you could have hammered them for their weakness. Nobody wins in that situation. Kindness, when given, is a win for everyone involved. Choose kindness and lend it to everyone who needs it. Is there a time you have lent your kindness to each other?

"You cannot be disciplined in great things and undisciplined in small things."

—George S. Patton

If you can't consistently make your bed every day and brush your teeth in the morning and again at night, there is little hope that you can put in the work necessary to be great at the "big" things in life. Share with each other the areas of your life you are disciplined and where you need to be more disciplined.

Date: _____

> "No one who achieves success does so without
> acknowledging the help of others."
> —Alfred North Whitehead

Famous basketball coach Dean Smith spent years shaping young men on the basketball court with lessons that made them champions on and off the court. One of the lessons he drove home to his players was teamwork and gratitude for those around you. He would say, "When you make a basket, always point to the player who threw you the ball. That applies to not just basketball but everything we do. No one makes it through life without many assists".

It's easy to look at the good things in our lives and the things we have been able to accomplish and believe that we accomplished those things on our own, apart from the many people in our lives who made those things possible. How do you point to and honor those that help you?

> "When you are good at something you'll tell everyone.
> When you're great, they will tell you."
> **—Walter Payton**

Be humble and stay humble! Don't advertise your accomplishments, and never brag about how good you are. Ordinary people use their time to praise and promote themselves; the great ones are too busy getting even better. Let others talk about your performance while you focus on how you will take it to the next level.

> **"Stinking at something new is the first step towards being sort of good at something."**
>
> **—Jake the Dog**

Nobody is born great at anything. To be good at anything, you must embrace the process of being a beginner before becoming an expert. The process will be the same for every activity in your life, from learning to crawl before you walk or skiing bunny slopes before mastering black diamonds; the starting line will always be where you stink before you are great.

"Your shot might be off, but your hustle never should be."

—M. Jordan

Whether it's taking a test or playing a sport, there will be days when your performance could be better. That happens to everyone in every arena of life. You will have days when you are just "off your game."

You won't be able to predict when those moments will show up, and you may be unable to prevent them. You can only control what you can control. And you can always control two things: Attitude and Effort! That's your hustle.

Date: _____

"Practice with your superiors, never your inferiors."
—Erik Liddell

It is said that you are the average of the five people you hang around with. People who hang with healthy people tend to be healthier. If you practice with average people, you will be average. As a rule, find the smartest, fastest, healthiest, and most adventurous and sit in those circles. Take your seat with champions and see that the conversations are just different. By their presence, they will push you to be the best version of yourself.

Date: _____

**"Every job is a self-portrait of the person who did it...
Autograph your work with excellence."**

—V. Lombardi

Every job you will ever do and every word you speak will be your
advertisement to the world of who you are. We are constantly
producing and reproducing our self-portraits. And each will have
your signature of ownership. Make sure that everything you do is
done with excellence.

Date: _____

_____

_____

_____

_____

_____

_____

_____

_____

_____

_____

_____

_____

_____

_____

_____

_____

_____

_____

_____

"Excuses or results."

—Arnold Schwarzenegger

In every area of your life, you can have a pocket full of excuses, or you can have results! You get to choose, but you cannot have both. If you want something, you will find a way and make it happen. If you don't, you will find an excuse.

**"Remember, the last thing to grow
on a fruit tree will be the fruit."**

There will be times in your life when you feel unfinished. And there will be seasons where you have a pile of effort and no results. Do not give up. Just because you cannot see the fruit yet, does not mean that things are not growing and getting prepared for the fruit to appear. Most people give up right before the fruit starts to show. Be patient and keep cultivating.

Date: _____

_____

_____

_____

_____

_____

_____

_____

_____

_____

_____

_____

_____

_____

_____

_____

_____

_____

_____

_____

_____

**"What is down in your well, will come up
in your buckets."**

My dad used to tell me, "Son, if you run into a jerk on your way to school, you ran into a jerk; if you are running into jerks all day, you need to check your heart because you just might be that jerk."

Out of the overflow of one's heart does their mouth speak. If there is kindness in your heart, you will be kind to people; If there is selfishness in your heart, you won't think about other people. If you have love in your heart, that love will come out in your actions, and if you have anger in your heart, that anger will come out and land on other people.

"Out of every 100 men, ten should not be there; eighty are just targets; nine are the real fighters, and we are happy to have them; Ah, but the one, one is a warrior, and he will bring the others back."

—Heraclitus

This will prove true in every arena you find yourself. It might be school or a sports team; it may be a company or a church group; and it might be a military or college campus. A few people will not belong. It will not be the right place for them. A majority of each group will be discovered as average, and some will rise to the top. But in every group there is one or a small and select group that stands out as top performers; the leaders and those that will set the standard for the rest.

You will have to choose. Will you be average or slightly better than average or will you be the one: the one that everyone looks to and who they measure themselves against?

"Wherever you have dreamed of going, I have camped there, and left firewood for when you arrive."

—Hafiz

If you listen in your quiet moments to the dreams you have in your heart, you just might hear the voice of your Creator whisper, "Go for it. Take the risk. Make it happen." He knows where your dreams can propel you, for it was He who has put those dreams in your heart in the first place, and He has prepared the way for the journey and for your arrival. He has also, like clues to His approval and excitement, left along the path all that you will need to make your dreams a reality.

Date: _____

"Anyone can find dirt on anyone; be the person who finds the gold in someone."

—Luke Knight (8 years old)

It takes no effort to find people's mistakes. They are on the surface and easy to see and even easier to talk about. Do not take the easy road. Make the effort to find the good in someone and choose to talk about that.

"Greatness is never achieved through imitation. Be real! Be You!"

Artists paint masterpieces and imitators make copies. People pay great amounts of money for original works of art, while copies of those masterpieces are sold at flea markets for pennies.

There will be only one Beethoven and one Michael Jordan. There will be only one of you in this world, and the world needs your masterpiece. Do not spend your life trying to be someone else. Give all your efforts to discover the masterpiece that is you.

Date: _____

"Trials and tribulations are mandatory in life; misery is optional."

No person is exempt from bad days. Everyone will have bad things happen in their lives. They will lose people they love and things they like. They will fail at things they hoped to accomplish, and some things will not work out the way they hoped they would.

You will not always get to decide what happens to you. All you can do is decide how you will respond. How you choose to respond is the only thing you have 100% control over when bad things happen. Will you give up; will you throw a mighty fit; or will you accept that something you did not like happened and then choose to control the things that are within your control?

Rainy days will come; puddles will form; and storms will ruin your plans. The best thing you can do in response is to learn to dance in the rain.

"I would rather have four quarters in my pocket than 100 pennies."

When it comes to friends, four quality friends will always be better than 100 average friends. Do not be impressed with the person who has many friends, be impressed with the person who has a few friends that are quality friends. Pursue having a few quality friends and avoid the need to accumulate a bunch of average friends.

Date: _____

**"Amateurs practice until they get it right;
champions practice until they can't get it wrong."**

—Unknown

Bruce Lee said, "I fear not the man who practiced 10,000 kicks once, but I fear the man who has practiced one kick 10,000 times."

Ordinary people are content to get a skill right a few times, while winners are determined to practice and then practice again until they are confident in their ability to get it right every time.

Be determined to perfect whatever skill you want to develop. Refrain from settling for getting it right a few times; be determined to put the work in until you cannot get it wrong.

Date: _____

"There are only two possible outcomes when you compare yourself to another person, pridefulness or jealousy, and both are without value."

You cannot aim to be the best version of yourself and simultaneously compare yourself to others. Doing so is like trying to hit two targets at once; you will miss both.

If you compare yourself to those around you, you will soon discover that you are better than some and not as good as others. You will think yourself a better person than those you are better than and will feel the need to chase those who are better than you. Instead of constantly comparing yourself to others, keep your eyes on one target, the target of being the best you can become.

**"If you hang around with four monkeys,
soon you will become the fifth monkey."**

Character matters. Who you are matters, and so does the character of the people you surround yourself with. Pick people who are kind and compassionate; Be friends with those who challenge themselves and have a great work ethic; and surround yourself with others who seek wisdom and listen to wise counsel. You will become like those you interact with.

"People grow by making choices (good and bad) and then taking responsibility for those choices."

Every person makes mistakes. You will be no different. You will make a series of good choices and have a fair share of bad decisions. Make it a habit of making good choices, but when you make a terrible decision, you must take responsibility for that choice.

The first response to a wrong choice is to own that decision. Be honest with yourself. If you are traveling east when you know you should be traveling west, you first must stop going east. Then, you are ready to turn around and head in the right direction. Own your decisions and be honest with yourself and those impacted by your choice. Everyone makes mistakes, but not everyone owns their choices. Be a person who owns their actions and grows as you do.

Date: _____

**"Your talent is God's gift to you;
what you do with your life is your gift back to God."**

—Leo Buscaglia

Every breath you breathe is a gift from God; every beat of your heart is a reminder that God has gifted you your life. Everything that you become good at is a gift from your Creator. None of us can save our life. The only thing we can do is spend our life. How we choose to spend this life will be our gift back to God as gratitude for what He has given us.

Date: _____

PROMPTS FOR KIDS TO ASK DAD

- ☛ What is your earliest memory of your childhood?

- ☛ What was your dad like?

- ☛ What did you love about your mom?

- ☛ What did you like/dislike about school?

- ☛ Did you have a favorite grade, and what made it your favorite?

- ☛ What did you want to be when you grew up?

- ☛ Who was your first best friend, and what did you guys like to do?

- ☛ What did you have as a child that kids today don't have?

- ☛ What do you remember about the houses you lived in as a kid?

- ☛ What is the scariest memory you have?

- ☛ What is the funniest thing you ever did as a child?

- ☛ Did you ever get in trouble at home/school?

- ☛ What were some of the traditions you had at holiday times growing up?

- ☛ If you could change anything about your own dad, what would you change?

- ☛ Tell me the story of your first crush.

- ☛ What is your favorite memory of your dad?

- ☛ What was your first thought when you found out I would be born?

- ☛ Tell me about your first car.

- ☛ Use this journal to tell Dad how you are feeling right now. You can trust him.

- ☛ Tell Dad the things you love about him.

- ☛ Respectfully challenge Dad to explain something you don't understand.

- ☛ Record memories you shared together. Share what you loved most about that memory.

- ☛ Tell Dad what you want to be when you are his age.

- ☛ Ask him what he loves most about your mom and how they met.

- ☛ Ask Dad to describe his friends and what makes a good friend.

- ☛ Tell me the story of how my name was selected. Tell me about your name.

Remember, one day, you will look back at all these entries and smile. This journal will be a treasure more valuable than anything Dad could have given you because he is gifting you a part of himself by doing this journal together. Make the most of it.

PROMPTS FOR DADS TO ASK KIDS

- ☛ Ask your child what they dream of becoming as an adult. Ask this often.

- ☛ What was your favorite part of this past week/vacation/ adventure shared?

- ☛ Express how excited you are for an upcoming trip/ adventure.

- ☛ Write about watching them at a practice – be positive and refrain from "coaching."

- ☛ Write about your favorite memories with them.

- ☛ Express how you felt when you fell in love with their mom.

- ☛ Ask them to describe what makes a person a good friend.

- ☛ Reflect on times you spent together – the things you loved about being with them.

- ☛ If your child is young, write down memories (funny things they did/said) for them to read later. They will love hearing about when they had a blowout in their diaper and how panicked you were.

- ☛ Tell your story to them. You will never find another human more interested in your story than your child. Tell them as much as you can recall.

- ☛ Write out questions that will make them think about what it means to be a good human.

- ☛ Write about your expectations.

- ☛ Express qualities they should admire in others, including their future spouse.

- ☛ Ask them about their friends.

- ☛ Encourage them to talk about their current friends.

- ☛ Share the most extraordinary adventures you have been on.

- ☛ Write about times you failed and how those failures shaped you.

- ☛ Ask them what their prized possession is. Ask this often.

- ☛ Ask them to describe their favorite foods or places to eat out.

- ☛ If you had one hundred dollars, how would you spend it?

- ☛ Ask what they would change about the world they live in.

- ☛ Ask them to tell you their all-time hero. Ask often.

- ☛ List areas in your life where I (dad) can be more supportive.

- ☛ Ask them to describe a perfect weekend getaway with you. Details, details, details.

About the Author

Dennis Knight, a pastor, speaker, and business owner, is passionate about men's ministry. As a pastor, speaker, and father for the past 27 years, he is establishing a new ministry that celebrates and equips men to become all God intended when He designed the masculine heart. Beyond writing and speaking, Dennis enjoys training in Jujitsu and hiking with his wife as they work to conquer all 48 of the 4000' peaks in New Hampshire.

Contact information is available through
www.kingme-ministries.com.

Printed in the USA
CPSIA information can be obtained
at www.ICGtesting.com
LVHW011247040624
782220LV00014B/826